This delightful Fireside book is the latest in a series that have been specially imagined to help grown-ups learn about the world around them. Using large clear type, simple and easy-to-grasp words, frequent repetition, and thoughtful matching of text with pictures, these books should be a great comfort to grown-ups.

The Fireside Grown-up Guides understand that the world is just as confusing to a forty-year-old as it is to a four-year-old. By breaking down the complexity of grown-up life into easy-to-digest nuggets of information, and pairing them with colorful illustrations even a child could under-stand, the Fireside Grown-up Guides prove that being a grown-up can be as simple as "look and remember."

The publishers gratefully acknowledge assistance provided by Josh Weinstein, Egregius Professor of Reference at Mars University and Reader-in-Residence at Springfield Library, in compiling this book.

THE FIRESIDE GROWN-UP GUIDE TO

THE
MOM

by J. A. HAZELEY, N.S.F.W.
and J. P. MORRIS, O.M.G.

Authors of *101 Dog's Eggs*

TOUCHSTONE

New York   London   Toronto   Sydney   New Delhi

This is a mom.

A mom has two very important jobs to do. One is to look after her children.

The other is to do everything else as well.

Being a new mom is full of wonder.

Sally wonders if her left shoulder will ever stop smelling of puke.

Gwen is having a little brother or sister for Shannon.

Gwen looks at all Shannon's old baby things and laughs. It seems so long ago. She has forgotten everything about babies.

This may be why she is having another one.

The mom gets lots of help from her little ones.

Daisy is helping to move the laundry basket away from her mom.

She has done this fourteen times in the last five minutes.

Eleanor and Simon have booked
their first ever babysitter.
They have a whole night to
themselves.

They go to a restaurant and talk
about whether the babysitter
can cope if anything goes
wrong.

The babysitter will be slightly
annoyed when Simon and
Eleanor come home at nine
o'clock.

Liz promised Oliver he could have some Sour Patch Xploderz if he stopped screaming in the supermarket.

She was so embarrassed that she left before buying any real food.

Liz tells herself that, if she puts the Sour Patch Xploderz on a plate with enough ketchup, they probably count as a vegetable.

The mom has sensitive ears that respond to the frequency of her child's voice.

The mom does not like hearing her own voice. That is because it does not sound like her voice anymore.

It sounds like her mom's.

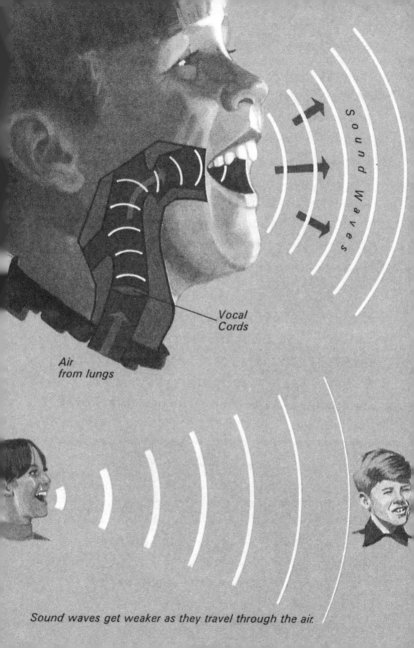

Sound
Waves

Vocal
Cords

Air
from lungs

Sound waves get weaker as they travel through the air.

Bella has made a den out of the laundry rack.

Bella's mom does not need the laundry rack. She has been too busy doing things for Bella to wash any clothes.

Bella's mom wonders what the record is for the number of days someone has worn the same bra.

The mom is good at making things from whatever is lying around the house.

Cathy made this doll from the corks of six bottles of Pinot Grigio that were lying around the house.

One of the things that is now lying around the house is Cathy.

Now that Lindsay's little boy is in nursery school, she is looking for a job.

At this interview, the lady asks Lindsay all sorts of questions, which Lindsay has trouble answering because she has the theme song from *Jake and the Never Land Pirates* going around in her head.

Lindsay hopes she is not singing it out loud.

Alice is a successful biochemist. She publishes at least one highly regarded academic paper a year and has won the Colworth Medal.

At the school gate, nobody knows this. Alice does not even have a name. Everyone calls her Olivia's mom.

Olivia has not done anything yet.

Heather hoped she might be like the mom in one of the fairy tales she read as a little girl.

But she is not good, gentle, and kind. She is weary, waspish, and resentful, like a wicked old stepmother.

Still, she did get one thing right. Everything in her home is covered with porridge.

Moms are everywhere.

In 1974, the Soviet Space
Agency landed a robot mom
on the moon.

MAMA was designed to collect
dust from the moon's surface,
using a reinforced silicon hanky
and distilled spit.

Lily's mom says waiting for things makes them better. She says Lily can have the toy car if she waits until Christmas.

Lily does not mind. She is spending this weekend with her dad. She will get the car then.

On Sunday nights, Lily learns all sorts of interesting new words from her mom.

The mom always carries a handbag. It contains important supplies and weighs as much as a microwave oven full of shoes.

Lara has a recurring nightmare in which the Handbag Police caution her for not having enough wet wipes or emergency bananas.

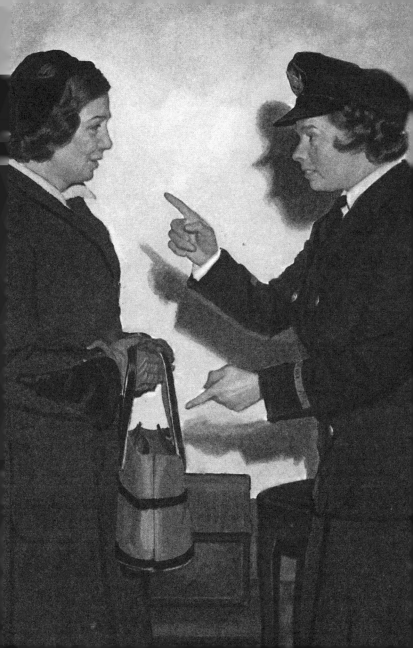

Sophie's son Henry has invited some friends around for a birthday party.

Afterward, Sophie finishes the children's leftovers. She is so full of ham, carrot sticks, pita bread, dips, and cake that she cannot bend over.

When Henry's dad comes home with takeout Chinese, Sophie puts on her what-a-lovely-surprise face and pretends to be ill.

Louise's cup of coffee is going cold.

There are six other cold cups of coffee on surfaces around the house.

When the vacuuming is done, Louise hopes she will be able to find the time to throw them away.

Julie said her children could have some pets if they promised to feed and look after them.

She has been too busy chasing Fluffy and Minecraft, the lizards, around the garden to get anything for supper.

"Lizard probably tastes a bit like chicken," thinks Julie.

When she was single, Debbie had nightmares about being left alone and unwanted.

For the last three years, someone has called for her every two minutes and watched her every time she has taken a bath or sat on the toilet.

Debbie now dreams of being left alone and unwanted, even for just a few minutes.

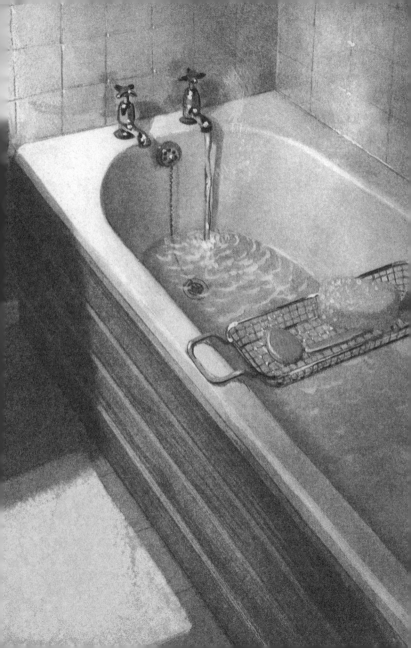

Tara's sister has come for dinner. She is talking about all the current TV shows.

Tara has not seen any of the programs her sister likes. This is because she goes to bed half an hour after the children.

She has seen *Thomas and the Magic Railroad* two hundred and eleven times, but she does not want to talk about it.

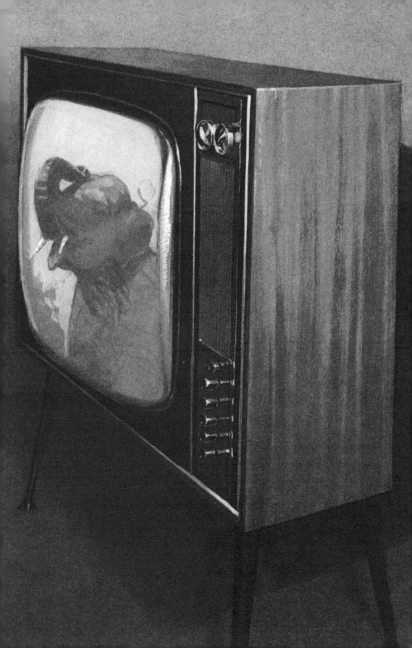

"Don't forget your scarf, Scott," says his mom.

Scott has not forgotten his scarf in years. He is forty-six.

Lisa has been shopping. She had a long list of things to buy, but now thinks she may have forgotten something.

Lisa is right. She has forgotten her daughter. She left her playing on an iPad in Target an hour ago.

Her daughter will still be there. She likes the iPad because it is not too busy to play with her.

The young kangaroo lives with its mom until it is strong enough to leave.

Unlike a human child, it does not move back in shortly afterward and stay for years.

Emily is cycling to work. She has already been awake for four hours because her two-year-old thinks wake-up time is 3:30 a.m.

The other moms at work will have lots of reassuring stories about how their children sleep through the night and have to be woken for school.

Luckily, Emily is too tired to kill the other moms.

TOUCHSTONE
An Imprint of Simon & Schuster, Inc.
1230 Avenue of the Americas
New York, NY 10020

First Touchstone hardcover edition October 2016

TOUCHSTONE and colophon are registered trademarks of Simon & Schuster, Inc.

For information about special discounts for bulk purchases,
please contact Simon & Schuster Special Sales at 1-866-506-1949
or business@simonandschuster.com.

The Simon & Schuster Speakers Bureau can bring authors to your live event.
For more information or to book an event, contact the Simon & Schuster Speakers Bureau
at 1-866-248-3049 or visit our website at www.simonspeakers.com.

Manufactured in Mexico

1   3   5   7   9   10   8   6   4   2

Library of Congress Cataloging-in-Publication Data

Names: Hazeley, Jason, author. | Morris, Joel (Comedy writer), author.
Title: The Fireside grown-up guide to the mom / Jason Hazeley, Joel Morris.
Other titles: Mom | Mom
Description: New York : Touchstone, 2016. | Series: The fireside grown-up guides
Identifiers: LCCN 2016011236 | ISBN 9781501150777 (hardback)
Subjects: LCSH: Mothers—Humor. | Motherhood—Humor. | BISAC: HUMOR / Form /
Parodies. | HUMOR / Topic / Marriage & Family.
Classification: LCC PN6231.M68 H395 2016 | DDC 818/.5402—dc23
LC record available at https://lccn.loc.gov/2016011236

ISBN 978-1-5011-5077-7
ISBN 978-1-5011-5078-4 (ebook)

THE ARTISTS

Martin Aitchison
Robert Ayton
John Berry
Frank Hampson
Robert Lumley
William Murray
B. H. Robinson
Sep E. Scott
Harry Wingfield
Eric Winter
Gerald Witcomb

THE FIRESIDE GROWN-UP GUIDES TO

MINDFULNESS

THE
HUSBAND

THE
MOM

THE
HANGOVER

If you benefited from the Fireside Grown-up Guide in your hand, look for these others wherever produce and ductwork are sold:

THE HANGOVER

Consuming alcohol lowers the body's reserves of vital elements such as iron, potassium, water, and bacon. Every unit of alcohol kills the equivalent of two inches of bacon, which must be replaced the next morning.

THE HUSBAND

The husband knows many things. For example, he knows how many stairs there are, in case he arrives home unable to see them properly.

MINDFULNESS

Alison has been staring at this beautiful tree for five hours. She was meant to be in the office. Tomorrow she will be fired. In this way, mindfulness will have solved her work-related stress.